PRACTICE MUSIC THEORY

FOR THE LITTLE ONES

BOOK B

Josephine Koh
& Florence Koh

Published by
Wells Music Publishers
29A Binjai Park,
Singapore 589831
www.wellsmusicpublishers.com

Creative Concepts
By Florence Koh

CONTENTS

The Semiquaver

This is a **semiquaver**.   It may also look like this.

This is a **semiquaver rest**.

$$\text{♬} \quad = \quad \text{♭} \quad = \quad \frac{1}{4} \text{ count}$$

Exercise

1.   Change the following notes into semiquavers.

2.   Write the semiquaver rest.

PICTURE FUN

Circle the semiquavers and their rests.

You can beam (join) 2 semiquavers together.

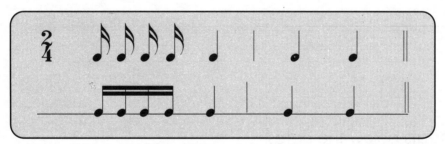

You can also beam 4 semiquavers together.

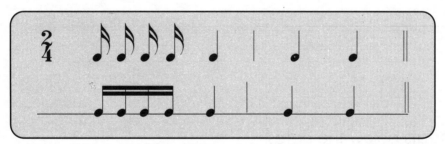

EXERCISE

Beam the semiquavers together.

Eg.

1.

2.

3.

4.

5.

6.

EXERCISE

Write the main beats below the notes.

1.

2.

3.

4.

5.

6.

7.

8.

The Dotted Crotchet

A **dotted crotchet** ♩. has $1\frac{1}{2}$ counts.

♩ + ♪ = $1\frac{1}{2}$ counts

This is a **dotted crotchet rest**. 𝄽.

Picture Fun

Colour each area with a **dotted crotchet** green.
Colour each area with a **dotted crotchet rest** brown.

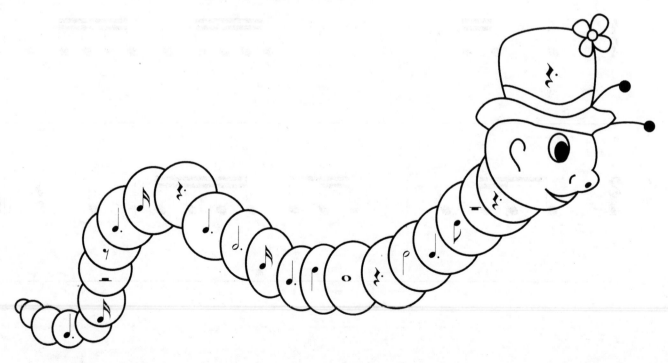

6

A dotted crotchet (1 $\frac{1}{2}$ beats) may be followed by another quaver or a pair of semiquavers to complete 2 beats.

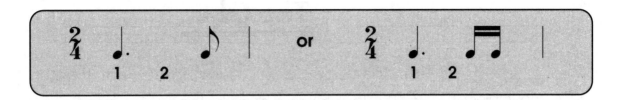

Sometimes a quaver rest comes after the .

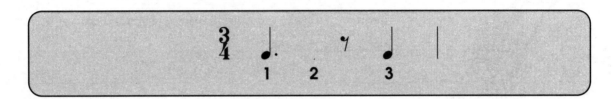

EXERCISE

Write the main beats below the notes in each of the following.

1.

2.

3.

4.

The Oboe

The oboe is a woodwind instrument. It has a double reed mouthpiece stuck into one end. The player blows air into the tube to produce sound. It is often used to play sweet and expressive melodies in orchestral works.

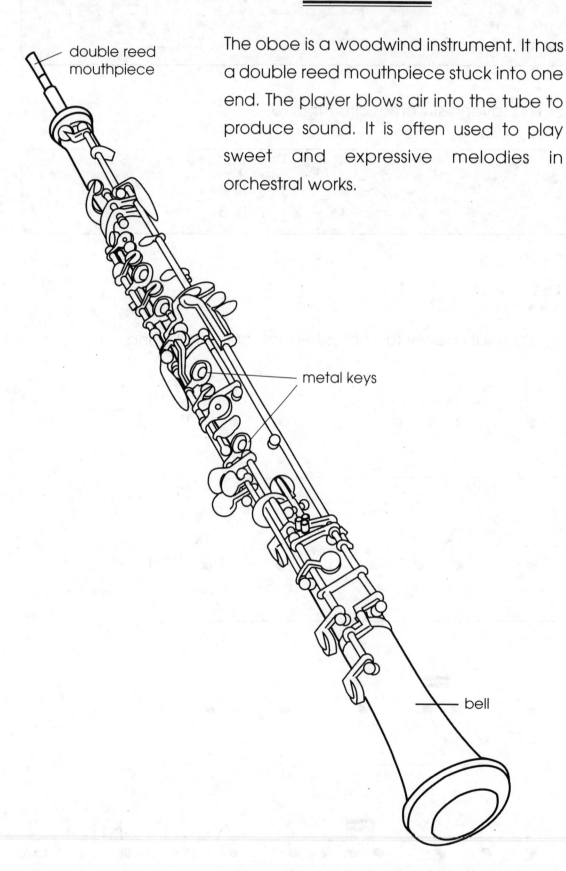

double reed mouthpiece

metal keys

bell

TIME NAMES AND TIME VALUES

Can you remember all the time names and their values? Here are all of them which you have learnt.

Name	Note	Rest	Value
Semibreve	𝅝	𝄻	4 counts
Minim	𝅗𝅥	𝄼	2 counts
Crotchet	𝅘𝅥	𝄽	1 count
Quaver	𝅘𝅥𝅮	𝄾	$\frac{1}{2}$ count
Semiquaver	𝅘𝅥𝅯	𝄿	$\frac{1}{4}$ count
Dotted Minim	𝅗𝅥.	𝄼.	3 counts
Dotted Crotchet	𝅘𝅥.	𝄽.	$1\frac{1}{2}$ counts

EXERCISE

Circle the longest note and then name it.

1.

_____

2.

_____

3.

_____

4.

_____

5.

_____

6.

_____

Circle the shortest note and then name it.

1.

_____

2.

_____

3.

_____

4.

_____

5.

_____

6.

_____

10

Circle the longest rest and then name it.

1. 𝄽. 𝄾 𝄼

_____

2. 𝄽 𝄾 𝄼

_____

3. 𝄽 𝄾 𝄾

_____

4. 𝄾 𝄾 𝄽.

_____

5. 𝄼 . 𝄼 𝄾

_____

6. 𝄽 𝄾 𝄽.

_____

Circle the shortest rest and then name it.

1. 𝄾 𝄾 𝄼

_____

2. 𝄼 . 𝄼 𝄼

_____

3. 𝄽. 𝄼 𝄽

_____

4. 𝄾 𝄽 𝄼

_____

5. 𝄽. 𝄼 𝄼 .

_____

6. 𝄾 𝄽 𝄼

_____

11

MATCHING GAME

Match each note with the correct rest and count(s).

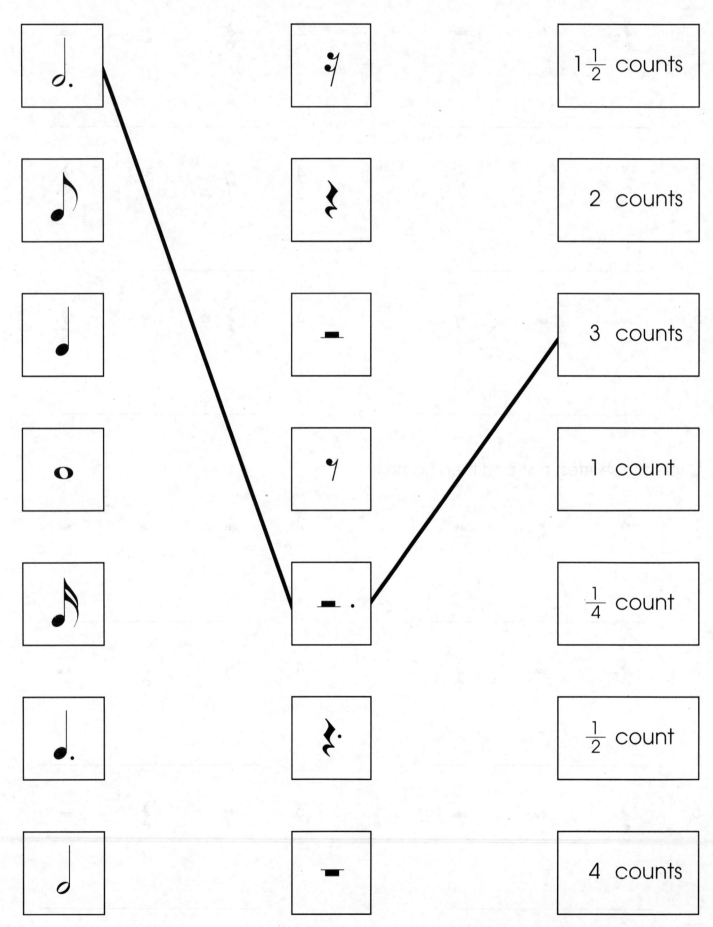

PICTURE FUN

Write the number of counts below the notes and rests in the picture.

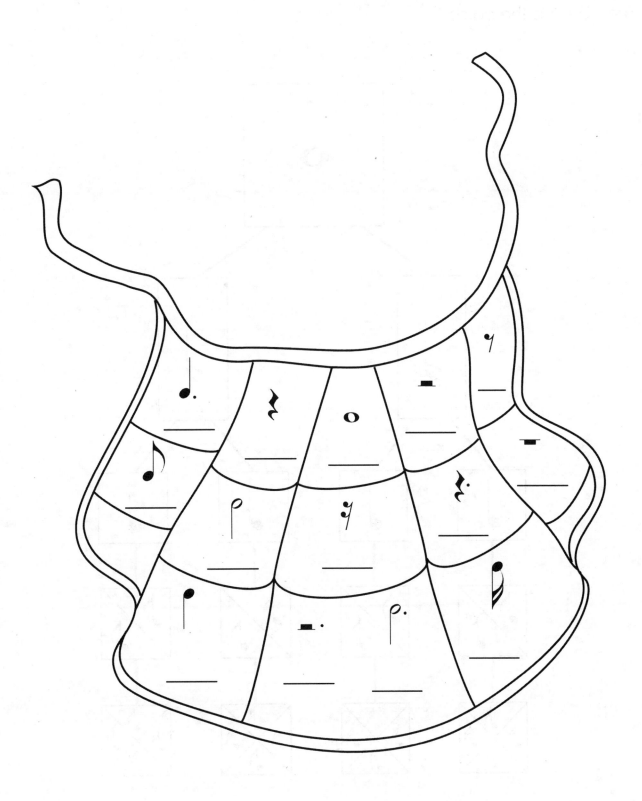

Use your Rhythmatics cards to form the picture below. The rests of these notes are printed behind the cards.

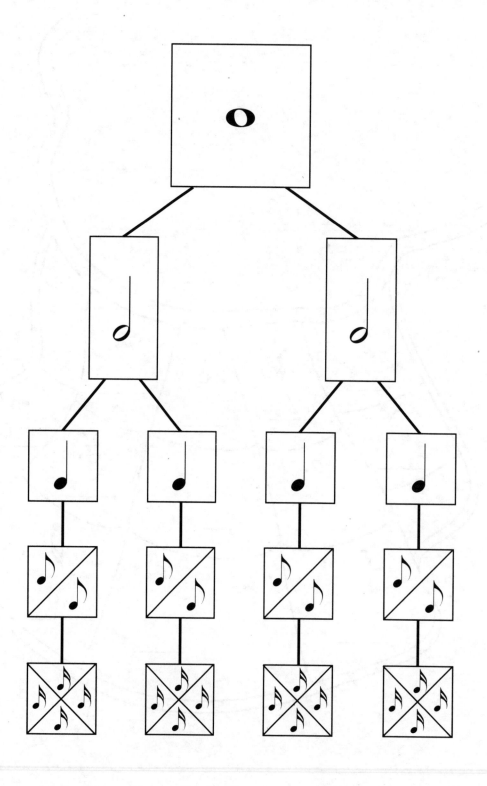

Exercise

∎∎∎∎∎∎∎∎

♪ Using your Rhythmatics cards, complete each space with the correct **note**.

1.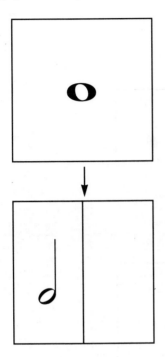

2.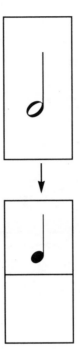

3.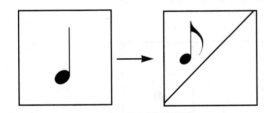

4.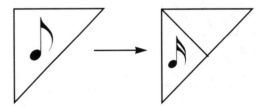

5.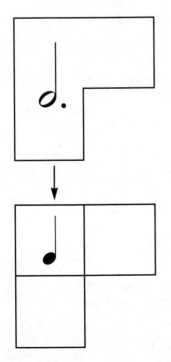

6.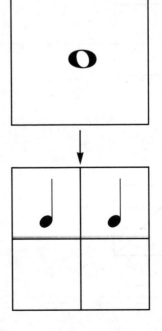

7.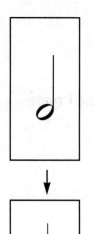

8.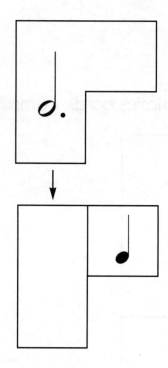

9.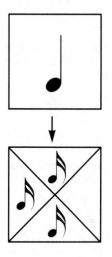

10.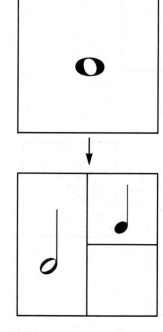

11.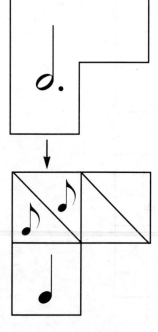

12.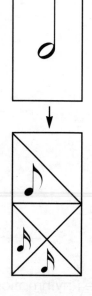

Rhythm Game

 Fill in each space with the correct **rest**.

1.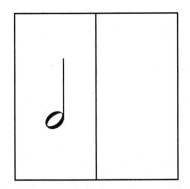

2.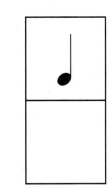

3.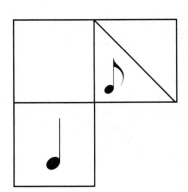

4.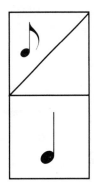

5.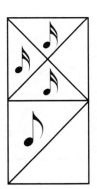

6.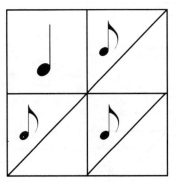

7.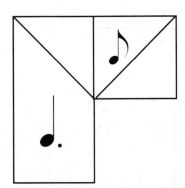

8.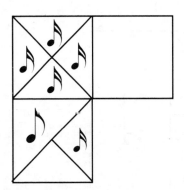

9.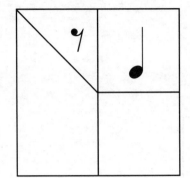

10.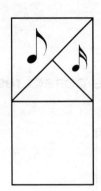

11.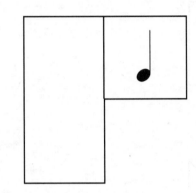

12.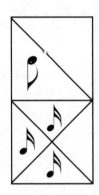

13.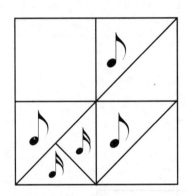

14.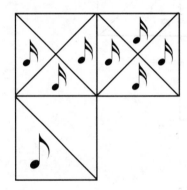

15.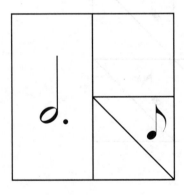

16.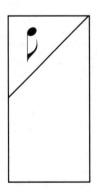

17.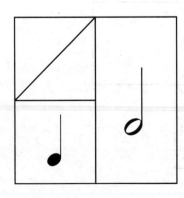

18.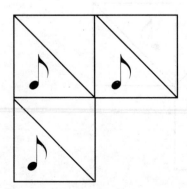

EXERCISE
■■■■■■■■■

♪ Fill in the correct answer in each of the following.

2 ♩. s   is the same as   **1** _____

3 ♩. s   is the same as   **1** _____

4 ♩. s   is the same as   **1** _____

2 ♪. s   is the same as   **1** _____

4 ♪. s   is the same as   **1** _____

6 ♪. s   is the same as   **1** _____

8 ♪. s   is the same as   **1** _____

4 ♬. s   is the same as   **1** _____

8 ♬. s   is the same as   **1** _____

16 ♬. s   is the same as   **1** _____

♪ Rhythmatics – How to Use Rhythmatics, Method 2

Here are the notes on the **treble staff**.

Learn to write and name them.

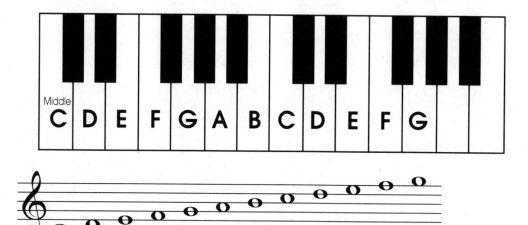

In Minims

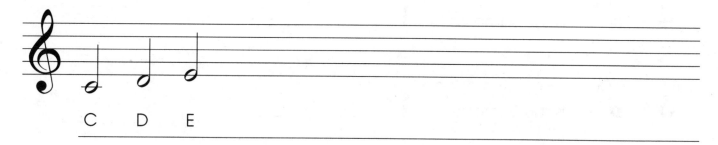

C   D   E

In Dotted Crotchets

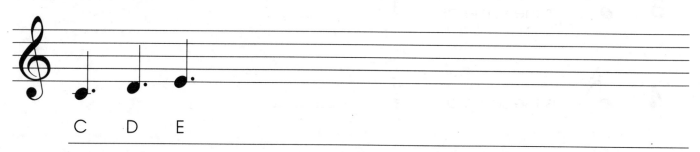

C   D   E

In Semiquavers

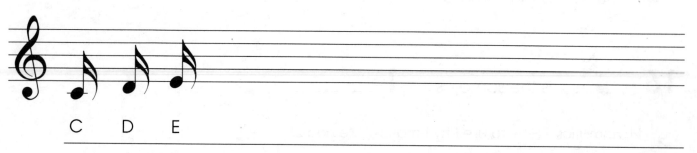

C   D   E

Picture Fun

Name the notes in the picture below.

The Keyboard Game

Write and name the notes that are on the keyboard.

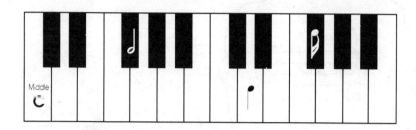 

F#   D   F#

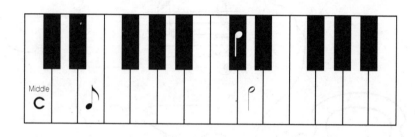 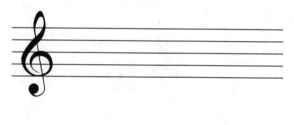

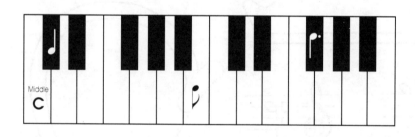 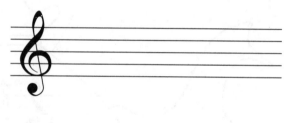

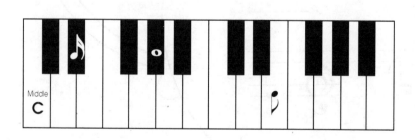 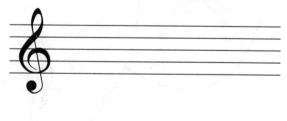

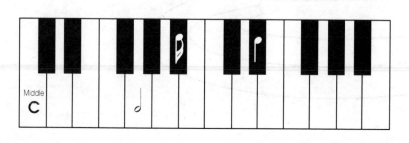 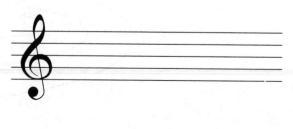

Here are the notes on the **bass staff**.
Learn to write and name them.

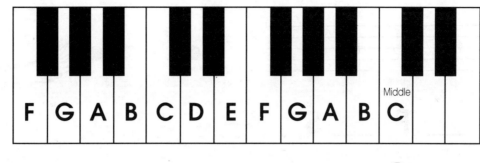

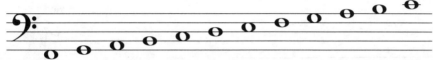

In Dotted Minims

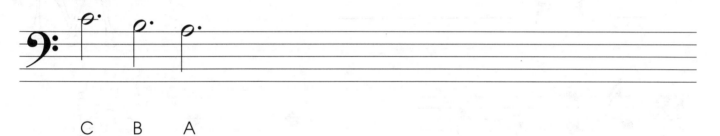

C   B   A

In Quavers

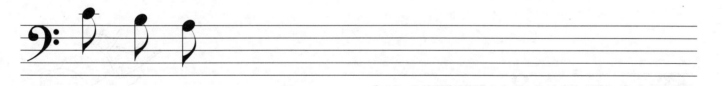

In Crotchets

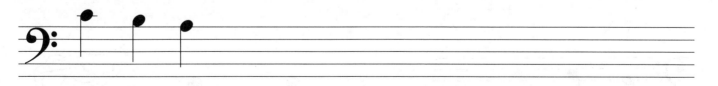

23

Matching Game

Name the notes, then match the words with the correct pictures.

_ R _ P _ S

_ I R _ _ _ _

_ _ K _

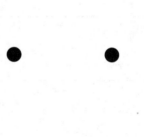

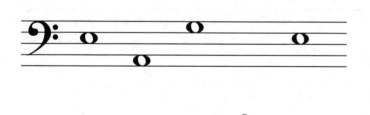

_ _ _ L _

_ _ _ R

24

The Keyboard Game

Write and name the notes that are on the keyboard.

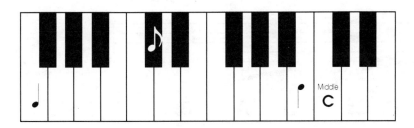

F

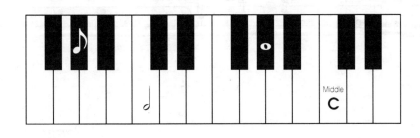
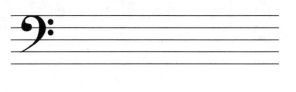

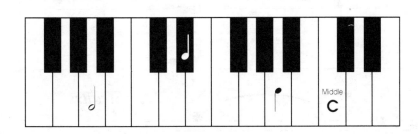
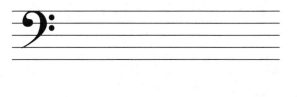

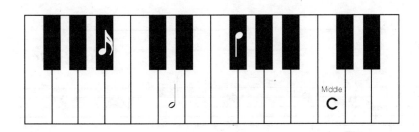
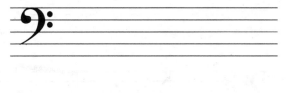

MUSICAL TUNES

Name the notes of these tunes.

F   E   D   C♯   D   A   B♭

26

THE TROMBONE

The trombone is a brass instrument. You blow air through the mouthpiece to produce sound. It has a slide which you may pull or push to produce different notes. It can play a fast sliding scale, called a *glissando*.

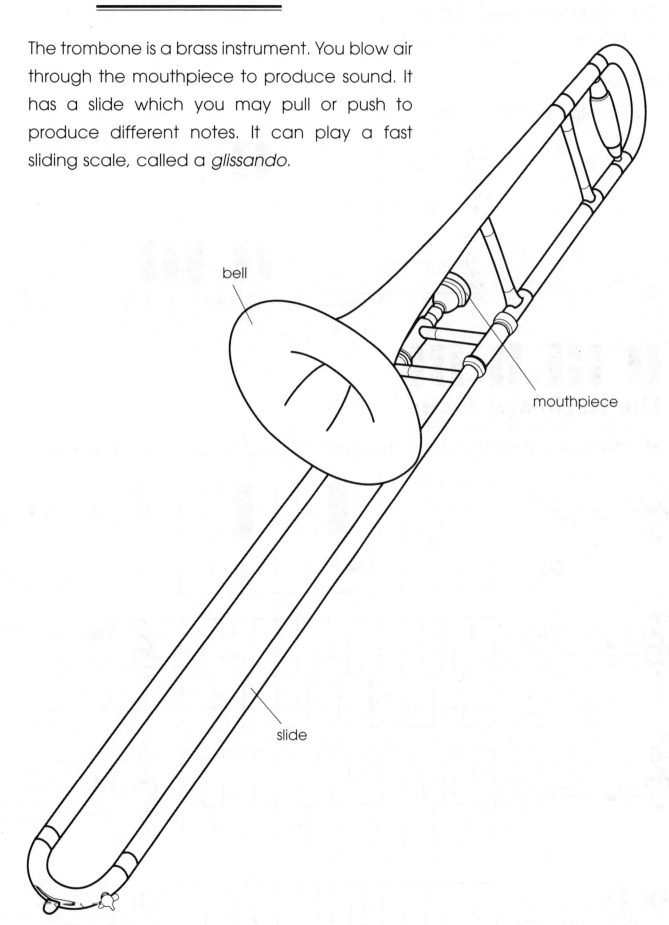

bell

mouthpiece

slide

SEMITONES AND TONES

Semitones

Notes *a step apart* form a **semitone**.

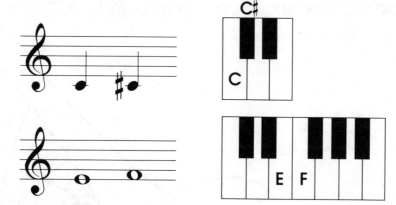

Write the note a semitone above the given one and colour it on the keyboard.

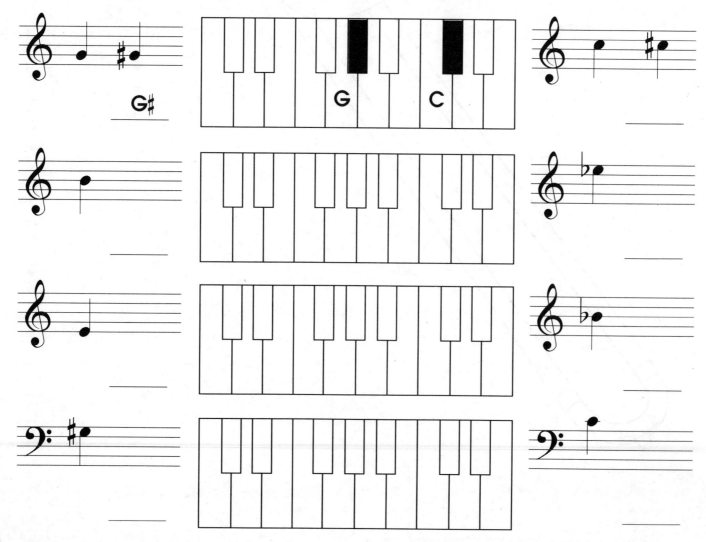

Write the note a semitone below the given one and colour it on the keyboard.

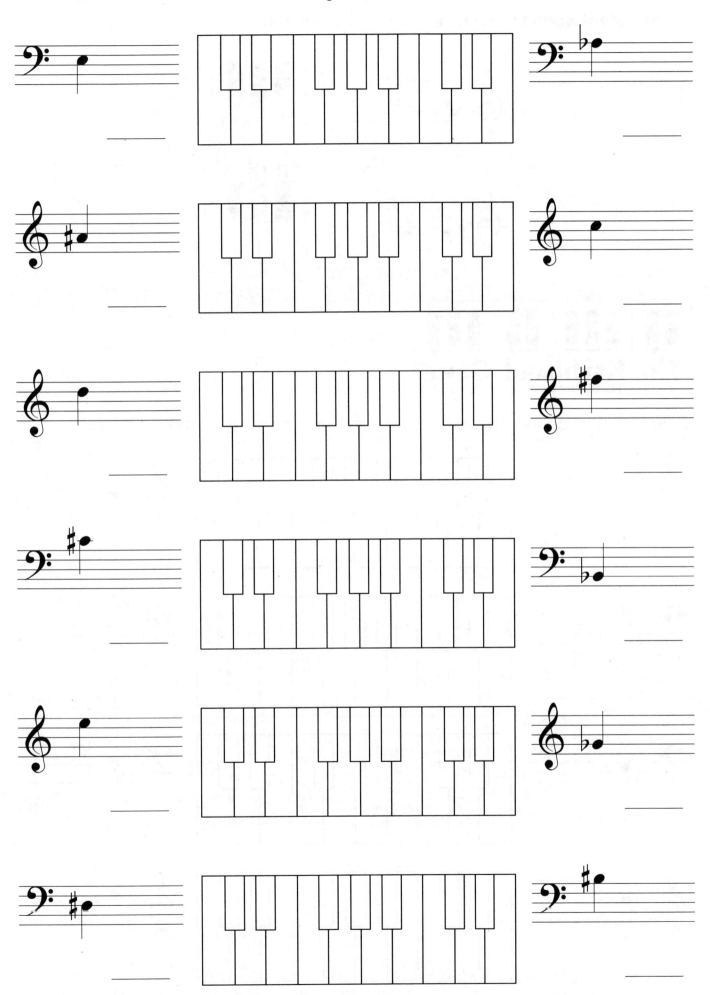

Tones

Notes *2 steps apart* form a **tone**. A tone = 2 semitones.

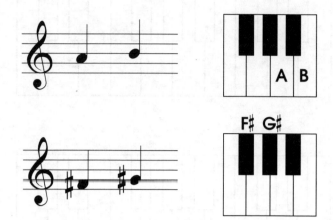

Write the note a tone above the given one and colour it on the keyboard.

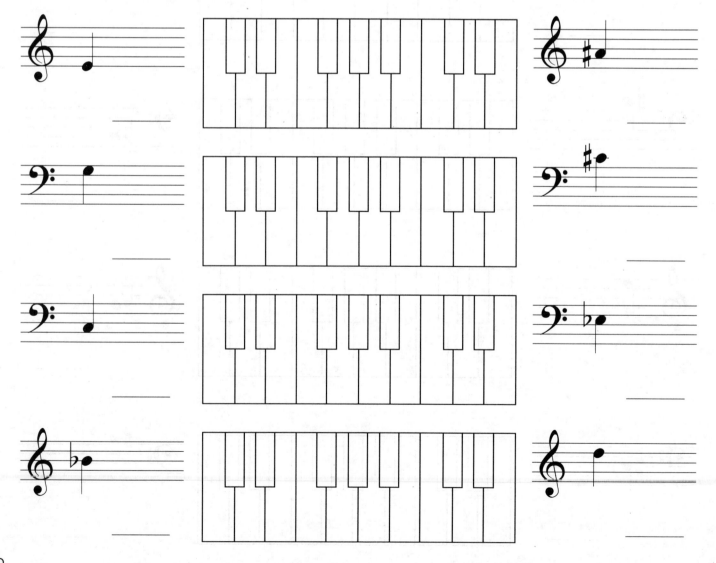

Write the note a tone below the given one and colour it on the keyboard.

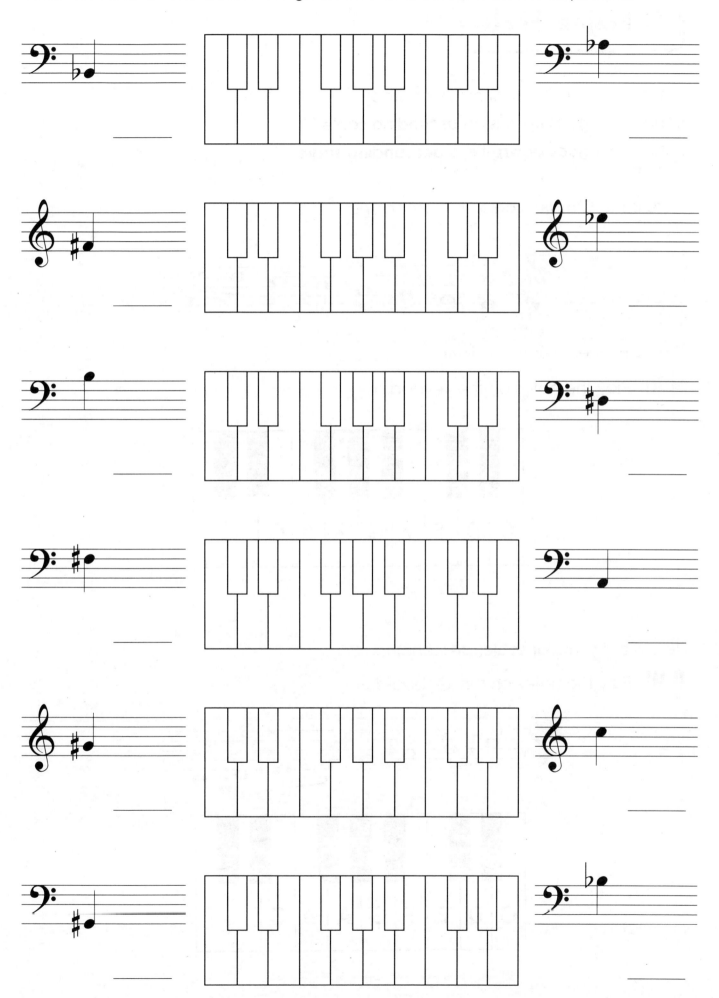

C Major Scale

A scale has 8 notes that move by step.

If the scale **goes up**, it is an **ascending scale**.

If the scale **goes down**, it is a **descending scale**.

Here is the **C major scale**. It is *ascending*.

The semitones are marked with a ⌐_____⌐ .

Play the notes on the keyboard.

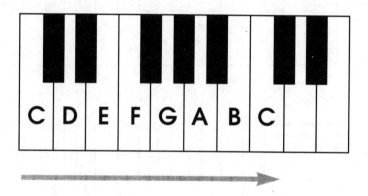

Here is the **C major scale**, *descending*.

Play the notes on the keyboard.

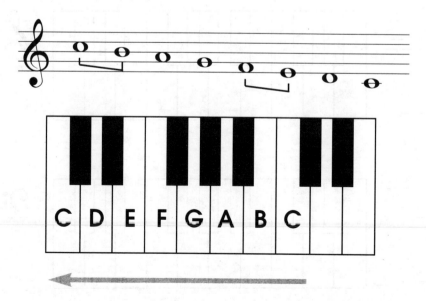

EXERCISE

Write the C major scale. Mark the semitones with a ⌐‾‾‾‾⌐ .

In **crotchets**, ascending:

In **minims**, descending:

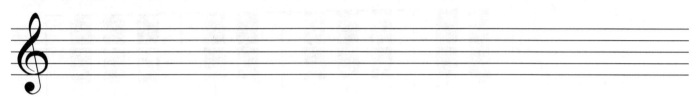

In **semibreves**, ascending:

In **quavers**, descending:

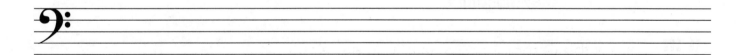

Mark with an " **X** " the notes of the C major scale on the keyboard.

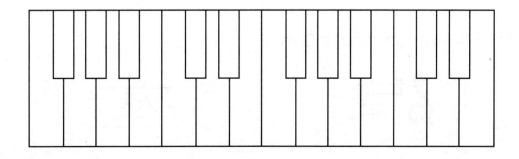

G MAJOR SCALE

Here is the **G major scale**. It is *ascending*.

The semitones are marked with a ⌐_____⌐ .

Play the notes on the keyboard.

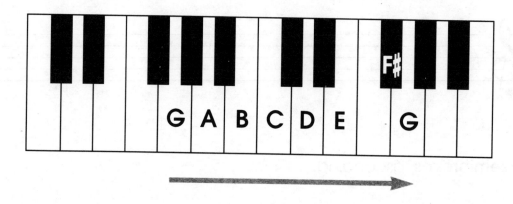

You may write the F♯ at the beginning, after the clef. This is called the **key-signature**.

key-signature

Here is the G major scale, with key-signature, descending. Play it!

Learn to write the key-signature of G major.

EXERCISE
∎∎∎∎∎∎∎∎∎

Write the G major scale. Mark the semitones with a ⌐▭⌐ .

In **quavers**, without key-signature, ascending:

In **crotchets**, without key-signature, descending:

In **semibreves**, with key-signature, ascending:

In **dotted minims**, with key-signature, descending:

Mark with an " **X** " the notes of the G major scale on the keyboard.

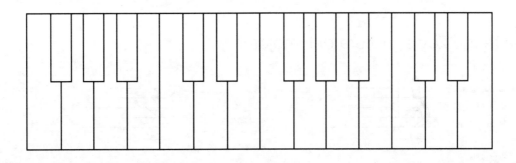

F Major Scale

Here is the **F major scale**. It is *ascending*.

The semitones are marked with a ⌐_____⌐ .

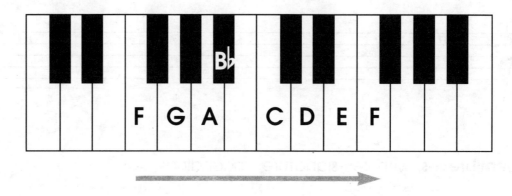 Play the notes on the keyboard.

You may write the F major scale with key-signature.

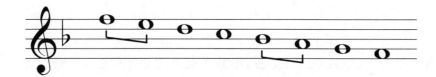 Here is the F major scale, with key-signature, descending. Play it!

Learn to write the key-signature of F major.

EXERCISE
■■■■■■■■■

Write the F major scale. Mark the semitones with a ⌊_____⌋.

In **semiquavers**, without key-signature, ascending:

In **minims**, without key-signature, descending:

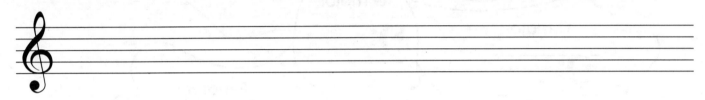

In **quavers**, with key-signature, ascending:

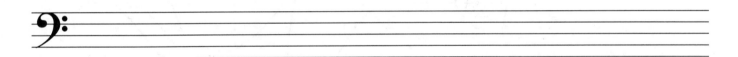

In **dotted crotchets**, with key-signature, descending:

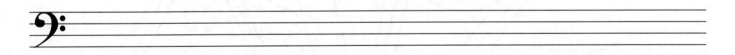

Mark with an " **X** " the notes of the F major scale on the keyboard.

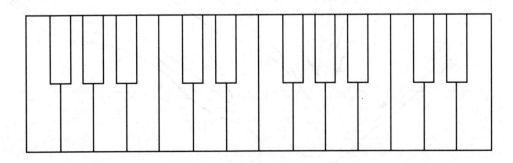

PICTURE FUN

Write the correct key-signature for the keys in the picture below.

EXERCISE

Add the accidentals where needed to make the scales correct.

G major

F major

C major

G major

F major

Name the key, then put the key-signature, where needed, to make the scales correct.

Key: _____

Key: _____

Key: _____

Key: _____

Key: _____

MUSICAL TUNES

Name the key of the following tunes.

Beethoven

Key: _____

Bach

Key: _____

Mozart

Key: _____

Haydn

Key: _____

Delius

Key: _____

The Timpani

Also called the kettle drum, the timpani is a percussion instrument with definite pitch. It plays one note at a time. You can tune the required notes by stepping on the pedal. Often 2 timpanis are used in the orchestra. But sometimes, 3 or more may be found.

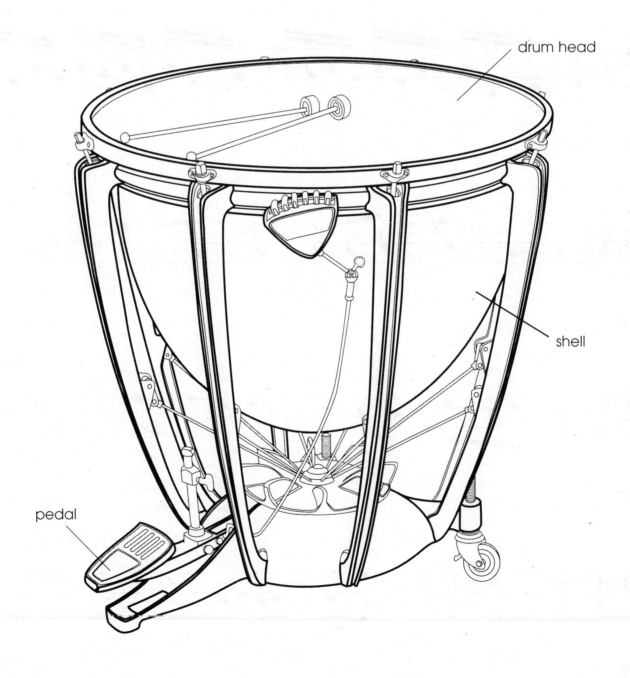

drum head

shell

pedal

The Tonic Triad

A tonic triad has **3 notes**.

They are the 1st, 3rd and 5th notes of a scale.

This is the tonic triad of **C major**:

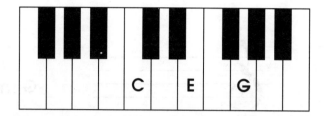

Here are the tonic triads of **G major**:

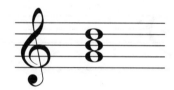

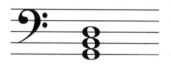

You may also write the tonic triads with key signatures.

Here are the tonic triads of **F major**:

Without key-signature

With key-signature

EXERCISE

Write the following tonic triads, without key-signature.

C major

G major

F major

Write the following tonic triads, using key-signature.

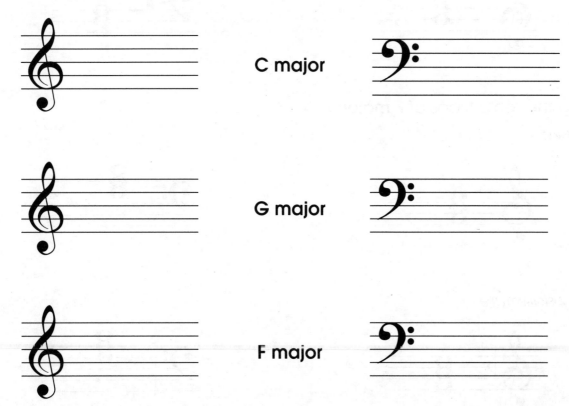

C major

G major

F major

PICTURE FUN

Write the following tonic triads.

(Can you guess the object below? Turn the book upside down for the answer.)

Answer: A biscuit.

THE KEYBOARD GAME

Name the key of each of the tonic triads and then colour the notes on the keyboard.

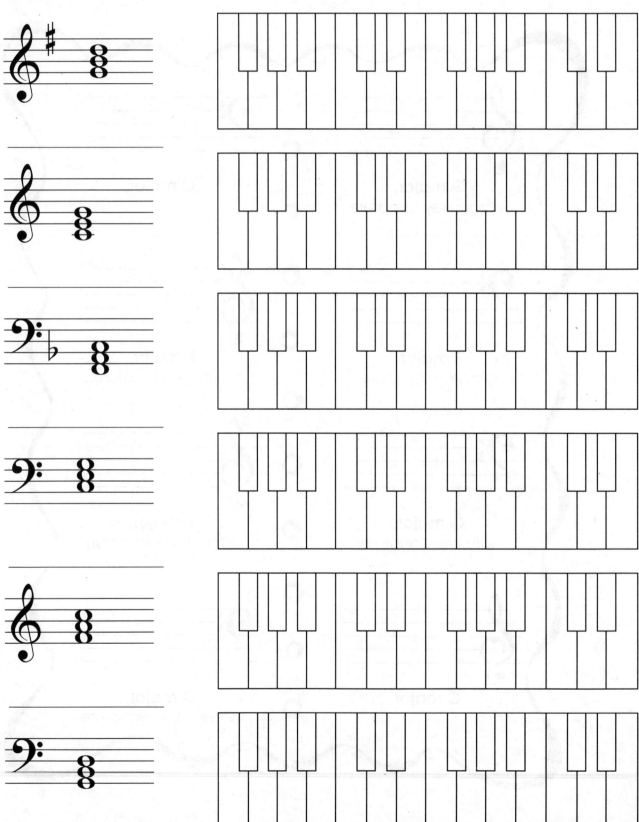

You have learnt to beam quavers:

You have also learnt to beam semiquavers:

Now, learn to beam quavers and semiquavers.

EXERCISE

Beam the quavers and semiquavers correctly. Then clap the rhythms.

1.

2.

3.

4.

5.

Rhythmatics – Refer to How to Use Rhythmatics, Method 3

6.

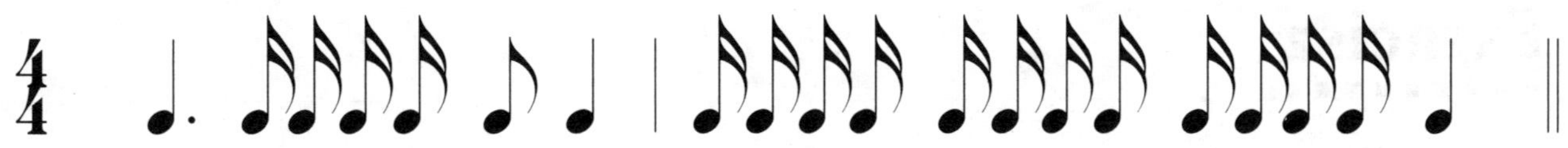

7.

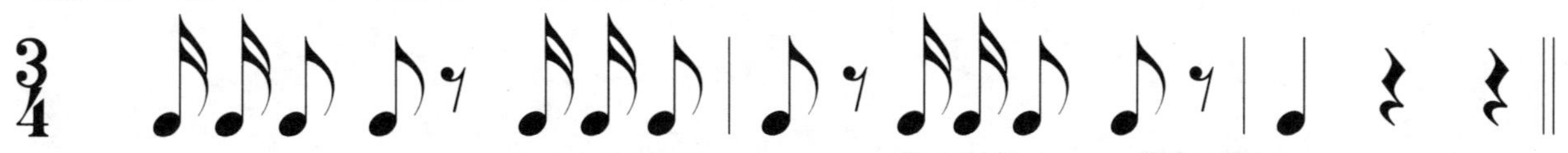

8.

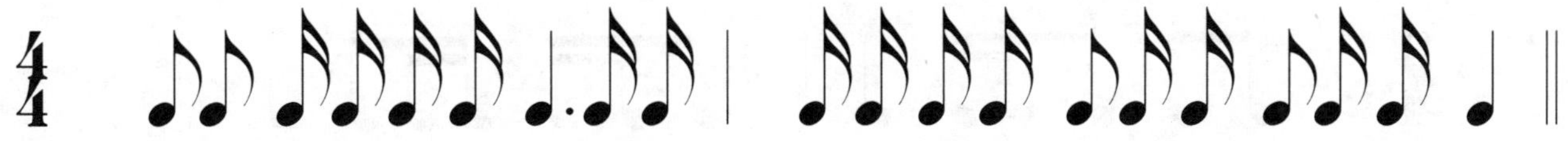

9.

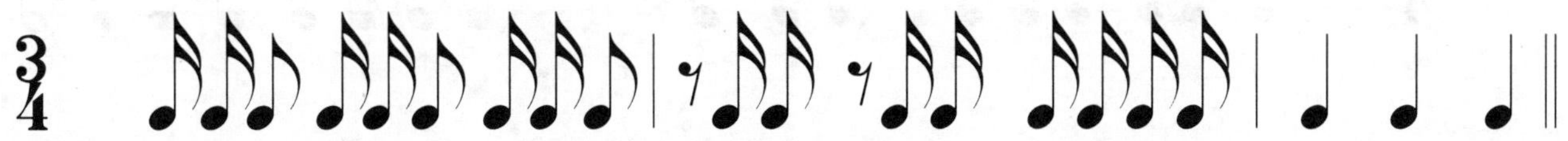

10.

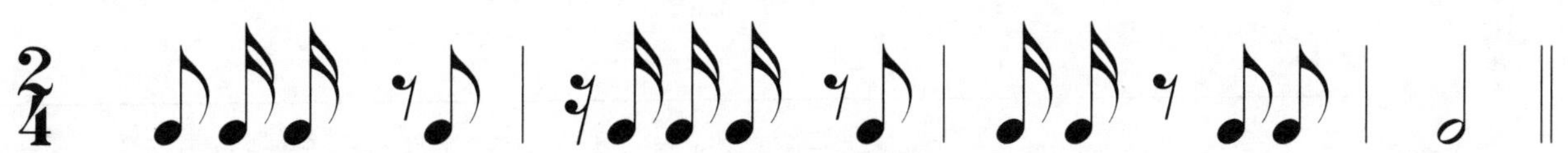

Exercise

Write the main beats below each of the following.

1.

2.

3.

4.

5.

6.

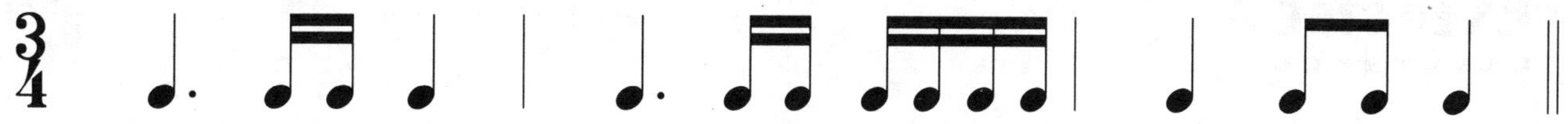

7.

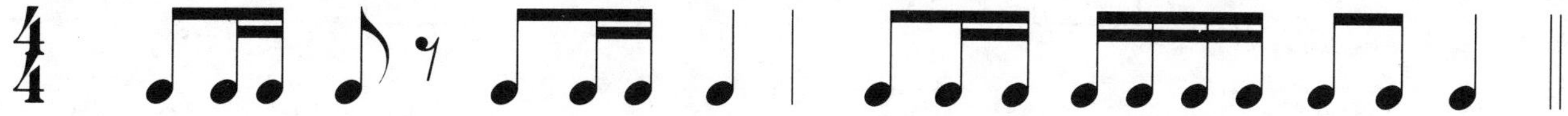

8.

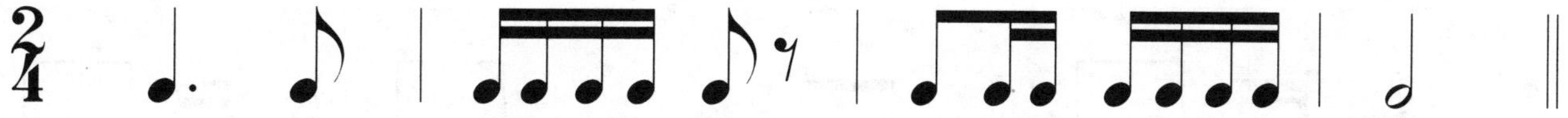

9.

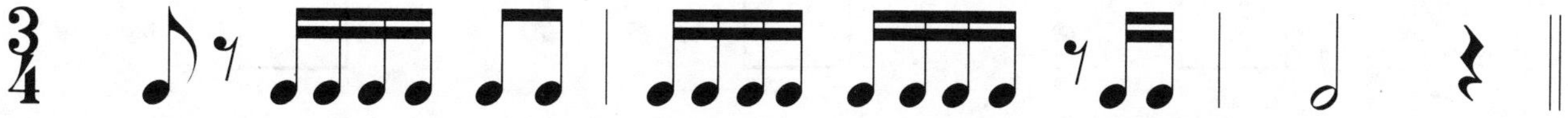

10.

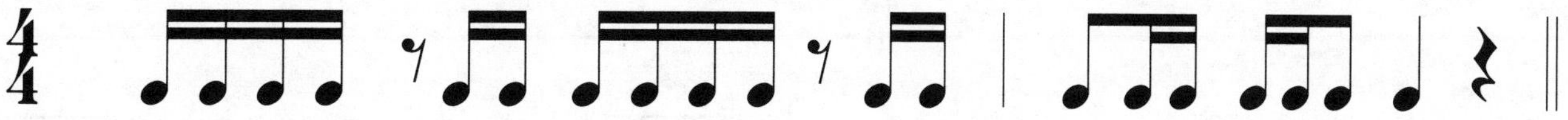

11.

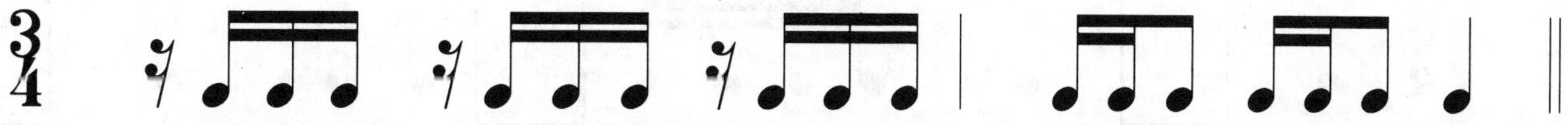

EXERCISE

Fill each ☐ with the correct note to complete the bars.

1.
2.
3.
4.
5.
6.
7.

Rhythmatics – How to Use Rhythmatics, Method 5

EXERCISE

Fill each ☐ with the correct rest to complete the bars.

1.

2.

3.

4.

5.

6.

7.

The Glockenspiel

The glockenspiel has a keyboard made of metal bars. It is a percussion instrument with definite pitch. This means that you can strike notes on the keys with hard-headed sticks. Can you imagine the bright ringing bell-like sound it produces?

metal bars

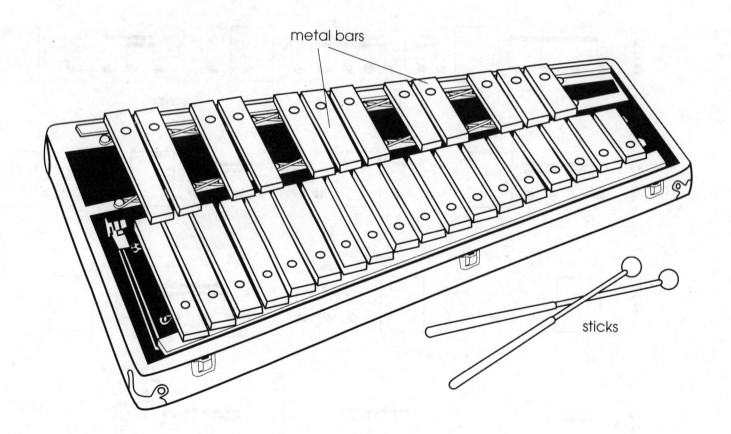

sticks

TEAMS AND SIGNS

Learn the meanings of these terms and signs.

p (piano)	Soft
pp (pianissimo)	Very soft
mp (mezzo piano)	Moderately soft
mf (mezzo forte)	Moderately loud
f (forte)	Loud
ff (fortissimo)	Very loud
cresc. (crescendo)	Getting louder
dim. (diminuendo)	Getting softer
andante	Slow
moderato	At a moderate speed
allegro	Fast
lento	Slow
rit. (ritard)	Getting slower
rall. (rallentando)	Getting slower

dolce	Sweetly
cantabile	In a singing style
	Accent
or *(staccato)*	Detached
	Long pause
	Repeat
	Slur
	Phrase
	Getting louder
	Getting softer
	Getting louder then softer

EXERCISE
■■■■■■■■

Explain the following terms and signs.

andante _____

cantabile _____

ff _____

pianissimo _____

< _____

dim. _____

p _____

mf _____

mezzo piano _____

𝄐 _____

𝄆   𝄇 _____

moderato _____

dolce _____

allegro _____

lento _____

rit. _____

mp _____

crescendo _____

𝅘𝅥𝅭

_____

> _____

𝅘𝅥𝅮𝅘𝅥𝅮𝅘𝅥𝅮𝅘𝅥𝅮

_____

p _____

rallentando _____

𝅘𝅥 (with accent)

_____

Matching Game

Match each sign or word with the correct answer.

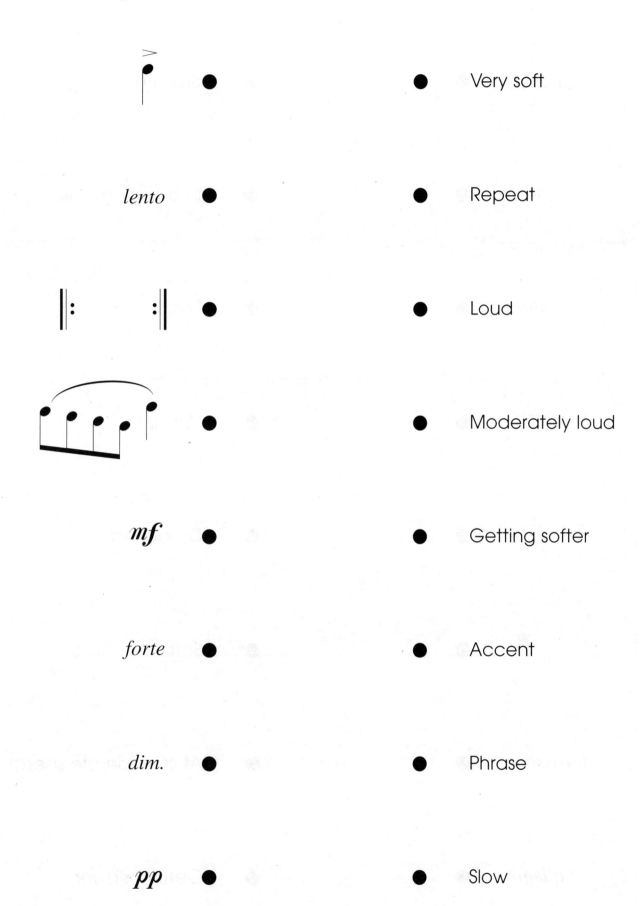

moderato ● ● Getting louder

cantabile ● ● Sweetly

piano ● ● In a singing style

ritard ● ● Fast

< ● ● Very loud

dolce ● ● Detached

𝅘 ● ● Soft

fortissimo ● ● At a moderate speed

allegro ● ● Getting slower

TEST

Total 100

1. Give the time name of each of the notes below.   **8**

_____   _____   _____   _____

2. Give the letter name of each note marked with a ✱.   **18**

Bartok
Dedication

_____   _____

Kabalevsky
A Short Story(Easy Piano Composition)

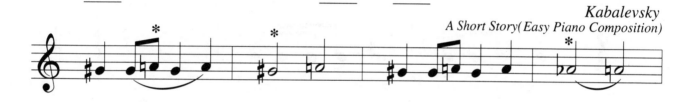

_____   _____   _____

© Copyright 1985 by Boosey & Hawkes Music Publishers Ltd Reproduced by permission of Boosey & Hawkes Music Publishers Ltd 1997.

Explain the following:

 _____    _____   _____

3. Write the following scales: **10**

In crotchets

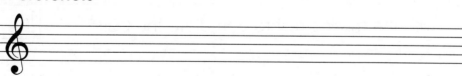

F major, without key-signature, ascending

In minims

G major, with key-signature, descending

61

4. Name the key of each of the following tonic triads.

_____   _____   _____

_____   _____   _____

5. Write the main beats below the notes.

_____

_____

6. Fill in each ☐ with the missing rest to complete the bars.

7.   Fill in the time signature in each of the following and then name the key.

Handel

Key: _____

Mozart

Key: _____

Mozart

Key: _____

Beethoven

Key: _____

Key: _____

Look out for

RHYTHMATICS

A revolutionary teaching aid for the Little Ones!

Simple yet exciting, Rhythmatics is all about teaching rhythmic concepts to young children.

For a little child, the difficult part to learning music is to grapple with the concepts of rhythm. Many children have not even learnt fractions at school, so counting and grouping of notes will be very difficult to grasp.

Now, the solution is here!

With Rhythmatics, you'll never have the problem of teaching time values, note grouping or simple counting to young children. Simply use the board and place the coloured pieces over it as in a puzzle and your little ones will learn music and mathematics, and still have loads of fun!

Uses of Rhythmatics

1. **To realise the value of each note or rest.** Place the notation on the white board.

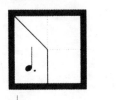

Thus ♩. = 1 ¹/₂ crotchet beats.   ▬ = 2 crotchet beats.

2. **To find the equivalents.**

♩ = _____ semiquavers.

Place ♩ on the white board.   Then place ◹ over the same area.

Thus, ♩ = __8__ semiquavers.

3. **To identify the time-signature.**

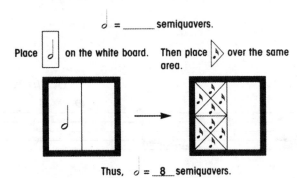

= 3 crotchet beats = $\frac{3}{4}$ = 4 crotchet beats = $\frac{4}{4}$

4. **To group a set of notes, beat by beat.**

5. **To write the beats below notes.**

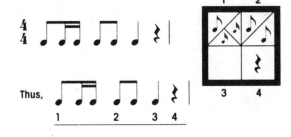

Thus,

6. **To complete the bar with the missing note value or rest.**

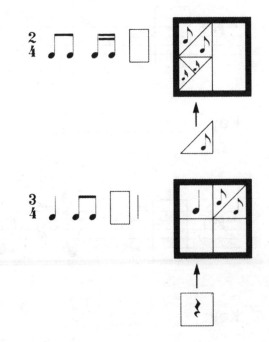